Summertime Sangria

A Collection of Awesome Sangria Recipes

to Delight Your Guests

Diana Loera

Summertime Sangria

Diana Loera

You are welcome to contact me at LoeraPublishing@hotmail.com

Please visit www.LoeraPublishingLLC.com for more books by Diana Loera and/or Loera Publishing LLC

If you'd like to follow me on Twitter, please look for @99CentsKindleBooks.

Thank you for reading my book. I hope you enjoy it as much as I enjoyed creating it.

Table of Contents

Introduction

You can take your Summertime entertaining up to a new level when you place a pitcher of sangria on the table.

Your Cinco De Mayo party may be well remembered due to the sangria that you served.

The combination of colorful fruit floating in a sea of red or white wine really adds to your table arrangement.

I've included recipes for red and white variations of sangria and I've also included two versions from Hooters.

You may be thinking Hooters? Years back, I had sangria while at a local Hooters and persuaded our waitress to share the recipe with me.

It was easy to make and could be easily whipped together quickly. I've served it numerous times for summer parties and until today no one has been the wiser regarding how easy the recipe is and that it originally came from Hooters.

I also included a variation of the original Hooters Sangria recipe – it has a few more ingredients.

I'm also including a Fast and Furious Sangria recipe – this is when you have zero time to prepare one of the more detailed recipes but still want a pitcher of sangria on the table.

If you like Moscato wine (my current favorite) you'll probably like the Peachy Moscato Sangria. Pretty as a picture on your table it just has summer elegance written all over it.

A word of warning regarding berries in the sangria recipes– I've found that they don't fare well if left to soak for hours or overnight. They often have a tendency to disintegrate in the pitcher.

With this in mind, I add berries to the pitcher right before serving (up to an hour in advance) versus the night before. Never use a metal pitcher either as it will give your sangria an icky metal taste.

Many of the recipes advise chilling for several hours in the refrigerator before serving. I agree that allowing time for the fruit to "soak" a little in the wine mixture does create a great sangria taste.

I also recognize that sometimes you don't have the luxury of the sangria mixture setting for hours. I've shortened the waiting time considerably by using chilled wine and adding ice to glasses with no complaints from guests.

In many cases you will see amount of wine listed as 1 bottle. A bottle is considered to be750 milliliter unless stated differently.

Regarding the type of wine you choose – you can experiment with different wines versus what is listed in the recipe. I wouldn't make your guests your guinea pigs but you can reduce the recipe for a glass or two and make it well before your party and try a different wine.

I'm a big Moscato fan and not a Zinfandel fan – you may be the opposite.

You also may want to experiment with garnishes – there are so many options regarding garnishes such as edible flowers - that will make your glasses stand out even more.

I'd love to see photos of your garnished drinks and you are more than welcome to email photos of them to be at LoeraPublishing@hotmail.com

Always check for food allergies before planning your party. You may have a guest that is allergic to strawberries for example.

Many people do not drink alcoholic beverages so it's always nice to have a non-alcoholic version on hand too.

I cannot stress this enough - please ensure you and your guests drink responsibly.

Garnishing

Garnishing your glasses can take a drink from great to wow as appearance is important.

Your presentation is an important part of entertaining.

It's really not that hard to take an extra step or two to garnish your glasses and the effect will be well worth it.

Garnishes can range from the traditional paper umbrella to a multitude of fruits or any clever stir sticks that have a motif to complement your party theme.

You can also use edible flowers or herbs.

A garnish, such as this flower, can make your sangria standout.

Food Pairing

If you are planning on serving your sangria with appetizers, you may be wondering what would be a good food pairing.

In Spain appetizers are referred to as tapas. If you are interested in finding out about tapas and some great tapas recipes please be sure to watch for my soon to be released book of tapas recipes.

In the meantime, here are some suggestions -

Cheese cubes – An assortment of cubes from basic Cheddar to Havarti to Pepper Jack accompanied by a variety of crackers.

Fried Chicken Livers – When dining at my favorite Spanish restaurant I always order the chicken livers tapas. In my opinion, nothing is better tasting than fried chicken livers with a glass of sangria.

Fried Calamari – Although like chicken livers, calamari isn't for everyone, it does accompany the sangria nicely.

Chips and Salsa – Create an array of salsas from mild to fire and maybe even a pineapple salsa. Serve with authentic chips 9I prefer the ones dusted with sea salt).

Fried Shrimp – offer a nice complement to the sangria

Barbeque mini ribs – the flavors complement the red sangria

Ceviche – another favorite of mine and it is a perfect match with sangria

Guacamole and Chips – Homemade guacamole really isn't that hard to make and nothing compares to homemade. If you do need to "cheat" grocery stores such as Whole Foods often offer a great guacamole.

There are numerous appetizers that you can pair with your sangria. Guests may enjoy homemade guacamole and salsa with chips. It's simple and easy to make yet goes well with sangria.

Kiwi Melon Sangria

Ingredients:

1 bottle (750 ml) dry white wine such as dry Riesling

4 peeled and sliced green kiwi fruit

1 peeled and sliced kiwi fruit (hold back for garnish later)

1 cup (237 ml) fresh watermelon, peeled, seeded and cubed (or to take this up a level you can create melon balls with a melon ball scoop)

1 lime, thinly sliced

1 1/2 oz. Midori melon liqueur

1/4 cup organic sugar (can use regular white sugar instead)

Combine all ingredients in a large pitcher (except the kiwi you will be using for garnish), stirring to crush some of the fruit. Cover and refrigerate overnight for at least 3-6 hours. Serve over ice and garnish glasses with kiwi slice.

Kiwi Melon Sangria looks and tastes very cool and refreshing. Guests will appreciate the beautiful color combination as well as light melon taste.

Cinco de Mayo Sangria

Bring the flavor of Mexico to your Spanish origin sangria with this recipe.

Tequila is potent and there are different varieties. I suggest starting with ¼ cup tequila and adding up to the full suggested amount depending upon your guests' preference.

Ingredients

1 bottle red wine chilled

1 cup Tequila

1/2 cup orange juice

1/2 cup sugar

1/4 cup lime juice

3 limes (washed)

3 lemons (washed)

3 apples (washed)

Directions

Mix the red wine, tequila, orange juice and lime juice in a sangria pitcher.

Add in sugar and stir well until sugar is dissolved.

Slice the fruit and add most to the sangria pitcher, holding some fruit back for garnish.

Put in fridge for 2-3 hours.

Pour into glasses filled ¼ full of ice and then garnish with leftover fruit.

Serve.

Spice up your Cinco de Mayo party with this Tequila infused sangria

Frozen Blood Orange Sangria Recipe

Ingredients

2 bottles dry white wine chilled (pinot grigio is a good choice)

2/3 cup cranberry juice

1/3 cup club soda

1/2 cup Cointreau or brandy

1 green apple, 1/2 chopped and 1/2 sliced

1-1/4 cups strawberries

4 blood oranges, juiced

2 blood oranges, peels removed and sliced

2-3 cups ice

Directions

Squeeze the juice from 4 of the 6 blood oranges. Place the juice in a large pitcher. Add the sliced blood orange pieces into the same pitcher, saving one or two for garnish.

Mix the white wine, club soda, Cointreau, cranberry juice, 1/2 cup chopped apple, strawberries and blood orange juice and pieces together.

In batches, blend the juice mixture with the ice until frozen. Serve immediately with apple slices and blood orange slices.

Cinnamon Stick Sangria

This recipe takes a bit more preparation and should set overnight if possible.

Ingredients

1 cup water

1/2 cup sugar

6 short cinnamon sticks

1 750ml bottle white wine

1 cup sparkling water chilled (hold until right before serving)

1 cup apple juice

1/2 cup orange juice

3 oranges (washed) Hold one back for garnish

½ jar maraschino cherries (about 12-15 cherries for sangria and additional for garnish if you choose)

3 apples (washed)

Heat the water, sugar, and cinnamon sticks until they're simmering. Allow to simmer for 5 minutes, and then turn off the heat. Let cool to room temperature.

While it is cooling, slice the oranges and apples. Remember, you will hold one orange back for garnish so don't slice until right before you are ready to serve your sangria.

Pull out the cinnamon sticks and mix in remaining ingredients except for the sparkling water.

Chill overnight or at least 5-6 hours.

Add the sparkling water right before serving.

Serve over ice and garnish glasses with cherries and orange slices.

Champagne Sangria

While this looks beautiful in a sangria pitcher, it is a very potent mix so please exercise caution when serving this beverage.

Ingredients

1 750ml bottle sparkling wine (chilled)

3oz triple sec

3oz brandy

2oz rum

2oz vodka

1 cup strawberries washed and halved

3 pears

3 oranges

½ jar maraschino cherries (12-15 cherries)

Garnish (optional) maraschino cherries, orange, lemon and/or strawberries

Directions

Mix Triple Sec, brandy, rum, vodka, strawberries and fruit.

Mix together well.

Allow to sit for 5-6 hours

Mix in the chilled sparkling wine just before serving.

Add to glasses ¼ full of ice and garnish.

Classic Red Sangria with Citrus

Ingredients

1 bottle dry red wine

1/4 cup lemon vodka

1/4 cup orange vodka

1/4 cup brandy

1/2 cup freshly squeezed orange juice

2 tablespoons simple syrup (you can buy simple syrup ready made at the grocery or make your own – recipe is below)

8 lemon slices, halved

8 lime slices, halved

Directions

Combine all ingredients in a pitcher. Refrigerate for at least 30 minutes before serving.

Simple Syrup Recipe

I've found this recipe to be much richer than store bought simple syrup so you may want to decrease the amount of syrup called for in recipes if you use this recipe and taste before adding the amount called for in the recipe as you may need less.

This recipe takes about 5 minutes to make. The batch can be stored in a well -sealed bottle for up to 6 months but I prefer to just make it fresh unless I plan on needing again in the same week.

Ingredients

2 parts sugar
1 part water

Directions

Bring the water to a boil.
Dissolve the sugar into the boiling water, stirring constantly.
Once the sugar is dissolved completely, remove the pan from the heat.
(Note: Do not allow the syrup to boil for too long or the syrup will be too thick.)
Allow to cool completely and thicken, then bottle.

A Classic Sangria adds color to your table and wows guests.

Fourth of July Sangria

Impress your guests with this red, white and blue sangria. It's perfect for Fourth of July or Labor Day parties.

Ingredients

1 750ml bottle Moscato wine chilled

1/3 cup sugar

3/4 cup apricot-flavored brandy

6 Tbsp. thawed lemonade concentrate

1 cup seedless red grapes washed and sliced

1 cup whole strawberries (washed)

1 cup seedless purple (blue colored) grapes washed and sliced

1 cup blueberries (washed)

Directions

Mix together the white wine, sugar, brandy and lemonade until well mixed.

Add in the red grapes, strawberries and purple grapes

Place in fridge for 5-6 hours

Add blueberries before serving

Pour over glasses filled ¼ full of ice. Garnish with American flags or other patriotic theme stir sticks.

If you do not have flags etc. you can always make a nice garnish with additional fruit.

Simply Melon Sangria

Ingredients

1 bottle Moscato wine chilled

1 melon (watermelon or honeydew) cut into bite size pieces

Lemon (optional) for garnish

4 ounces Midori liqueur (optional)

Directions

Mix ingredients and let sit in fridge for 2-5 hours.

Pour over glasses filled ¼ with ice, garnish and serve.

Simply Mango Sangria

Ingredients

1 bottle Moscato wine chilled

3 mangoes cut into bite size pieces

Lemon (optional) for garnish

4 ounces Grand Marnier (optional)

Directions

Mix ingredients and let sit in fridge for 2-5 hours.

Pour over glasses filled ¼ with ice, garnish and serve.

White Sangria with Pears

Ingredients

1 bottle dry white wine chilled

1-1/4 cups pear juice

1/4 cup brandy

1 cup chopped canned pears

1 cup chopped canned peaches

8 orange slices, halved

Directions

Combine all ingredients in a pitcher. Refrigerate for at least 30 minutes before serving.

White sangria is gaining in popularity.

Rosé Sangria with Limoncello

Ingredients

1 bottle rosé wine chilled

1/2 cup Limoncello or other lemon liqueur

1/4 cup brandy

1/2 cup lemon-lime soda

1 tablespoon lemon juice

1 cup sliced strawberries

Whole strawberries (for garnish)

5 lemons sliced (you will be holding back 1 lemon for garnish)

Directions

Combine all ingredients in a pitcher (except for lemon and strawberries you are holding back for garnish. Refrigerate for at least 30 minutes before serving. Serve over ice and garnish glasses with a whole strawberry and lemon slice.

Summer in a Glass - Peachy Moscato Sangria

This is a great summertime drink. The peaches really work well with the Moscato. You can eliminate or decrease the brandy if you wish.

Ingredients

4 (750 milliliter) bottles of Moscato wine chilled

4 (12 fluid ounce) cans or bottles lemon lime soda (such as Sprite or 7Up)

1 cup brandy

1 cup peach schnapps

2 fresh peaches, pitted and sliced

1 (16 ounce) package fresh strawberries sliced

2 mangos - peeled, seeded, and sliced

1/2 fresh pineapple - peeled, cored and cut into chunks

1 (6 ounce) container fresh raspberries

Directions

Stir the moscato wine, lemon-lime soda, brandy, peach schnapps, peaches, strawberries, mangos, pineapple chunks, and raspberries together in a large container and chill 6-8 hours.

Pour over ice when ready to serve.

Serve with a garnish such as a peach wedge, pineapple wedge or strawberry. You can also jazz up your glass with the famous paper umbrella.

Fast & Furious Sangria

As much as you may like the sangria recipes in this book, there may come a time where you have zero time and/or your budget calls for a less extensive shopping list. With this in mind – you can easily create a table worthy sangria.

1 jug (or bottle) sangria wine (chilled if possible)

Ice

A mix of at least two of the below fruits (washed):

Lemons

Limes

Oranges

Apples

Peaches

Strawberries (hulled)

Pineapple (cored)

Blueberries

You will cut up the fruit (except the blueberries). The strawberries you'll cut in half.

Quite simply, you'll put your fruit in a pitcher and pour the sangria wine over the fruit.

If at all possible, let the sangria and fruit sit for 30 minutes to an hour in the fridge.

You'll then pour your mixture into glasses (prefilled one quarter to one third with ice).

Garnishing of the glasses is really important. You can either put some fruit on the rim or if you have wooden shish-ka-bob skewers, put some fruit on as many as you have glasses and insert into the sangria.

Needless to say, this isn't as spectacular as the other recipes in this book but it works and is better than nothing if you've been invited at the last minute to a Cinco de Mayo party or if people have dropped in and are now staying for supper. You can easily create this sangria with fruit you may already have on hand. It's less expensive than making mixed drinks for everyone and it still looks classy on the table. No one besides you will know how easy it was to make.

Ginger Brunch Sangria

This sangria recipe is perfect for Sunday summer brunch when the sun is getting hot and you'd like something refreshing and fruit-laden.

Ingredients:

1 Bottle of red wine chilled
1 Lemon cut into wedges
1 Orange cut into wedges
1 Lime cut into wedges
2 Tbsp. sugar
Splash of orange juice or lemonade
2 Shots of gin or triple sec (optional)
1 Cup of raspberries or strawberries (may use thawed or frozen)
1 Small can of diced pineapples (with juice)
4 Cups ginger ale

Directions

Pour wine into a large pitcher and squeeze the juice wedges from the lemon, orange and lime into the wine.

Toss in the fruit wedges and pineapple then add sugar, orange juice and gin.

Chill 5-6 hours (can chill overnight if needed).

Add ginger ale, berries and ice just before serving.

Tropical Sangria I

Ingredients

1 bottle Moscato chilled
1 cup light rum
1/2 cup passion fruit nectar
1/2 cup Lemongrass Simple Syrup, or to taste, recipe follows
1 fresh lemon, halved and thinly sliced
1 fresh orange, halved and thinly sliced
1 bunch fresh mint leaves
1 fresh passion fruit, seeds removed (optional)

Directions

Combine the Moscato, rum, nectar, Lemongrass Simple Syrup, lemons, oranges, mint and passion fruit if desired in a pitcher. Cover and refrigerate for at least 2 hours and up to 24 hours.

Lemongrass Simple Syrup

Ingredients

1 cup sugar
1 stalk lemongrass, cut into thirds
1 cup water

Directions

Combine 1 cup water and the sugar in a small saucepan. Press on the stalks with the back of a knife to lightly bruise and help release the flavor.

Add the stalks to the pan and bring to a boil over high heat.

Cook until the sugar is completely dissolved.

Remove from the heat, cover and refrigerate for at least 1 hour and up to 48 hours to let the flavor immerge.

Strain before using.

Recipe makes 1 cup.

Tropical Sangria II (fast version)

This is the fast version for a Tropical Sangria

Ingredients
I bottle Moscato white wine
Up to1 cup total of Pineapple and/or coconut rum (to taste)
Pineapple chunks
Grapes (seedless)
Lime slices

Directions
Fill pitcher ¼ full of ice and pour above mixture over ice. If possible let the mixture sit in fridge for 30 minutes to an hour before serving.

Garnish with skewers of pineapple, mangoes and grapes and/or a paper umbrella.

Pineapple Sangria

Ingredients

1 750 ml bottle of white wine chilled
1 medium orange sliced into wedges
½ jar maraschino cherries (approximately 15 cherries)
1 lemon sliced into wedges
1 fresh pineapple sliced and diced to your preference (may use canned pineapple, substitute two 15.5 oz. cans of crushed or sliced pineapple)
1/4 cup of sugar
4 cups of ginger ale
3 shots of coconut rum

Directions

Pour wine into a large pitcher and squeeze the juice wedges from the lemon and orange into the white wine.
Toss in the lemon and oranges wedges (leaving out seeds if possible), cherries and pineapple then add sugar.
Chill 2-5 hours
Add ginger ale, rum and ice just before serving.
Garnish with a skewer of fruit.

The color and presentation of your Pineapple sangria pops with the addition of cherries. In this sangria we also added grapes and some lemon wedges. You can experiment with your fruit additions – and as you see the presentation can be spectacular.

These glasses weren't garnished yet .Once they are done will really add to the presentation.

Pineapple sangria can also be garnished with additional cherries, strawberries, edible flowers or herbs for an added pop of color. You can experiment with straw types and colors too.

Saturday Night Cook Out White Sangria

This sangria recipe creates a white sangria. White sangria is becoming more and more popular. You can still use red wine instead of white if you choose though. You'll be creating a beautiful medley of fruits that look awesome when swirling in your glass sangria pitcher.

Ingredients

1 Bottle of your favorite white wine chilled (you can use a red wine if you choose)
3 Lemons cut into wedges
3 Oranges cut into wedges
3 Limes cut into wedges
2 Peaches cut into wedges
1 cup sliced strawberries
1/2 cup lemonade or limeade
1/2 cup sugar
2 shots of apricot, peach or "berry" flavored brandy
2 cups ginger ale
Optional: one can of diced pineapple pieces with juice

Directions

Pour the wine in the sangria pitcher.
Squeeze the juice wedges from one lemon, one orange and one lime into the wine.
Discard squeezed fruit wedges.
Add in most of the remaining the fruit wedges (leaving out seeds if possible) and add sliced peaches, strawberries limeade/lemonade, sugar and brandy.
Chill for 2 to 6 hours if possible.
Garnish glasses with remaining fruit (if any fruit is left after garnishing glasses you can add it into the sangria).
 Add ginger ale and ice to the pitcher just before serving.
Pour into garnishes glasses.

Hooters Style Sangria

Ingredients

2 bottles of red wine (chilled)
Lime wedges (8 limes)
Orange wedges (4 oranges)
2 teaspoons sugar
1 liter bottle of 7up (you can use Sprite or Mountain Dew also)
Ice

Directions

Squeeze the juice from 1 lime and 1 orange into the sangria pitcher. Discard the squeezed fruit.
Cut the remaining fruit into wedges or wheels.
Add 2 teaspoons sugar to the mix and stir thoroughly.
Add ice to cover ¼ of pitcher.
Add soda and stir.
Add wine and stir again
Add ¾ of remaining fruit to pitcher and stir.
Save remaining fruit for garnish.
Store in fridge and serve. I make this in advance and let it sit in the fridge for an hour to three hours before serving.
You can hold the soda back until you are closer to ready to serve and add it in then (just make sure the soda is well chilled). Your main focus is allowing enough time for the fruit to mix with the wine.

Hooters Style Sangria Version 2

(Makes much larger quantity than version 1 and has additional ingredients)

Ingredients

2 Jugs of Burgundy Wine (chilled)

2 liter(s) of 7-up

2 liter(s) of Mountain Dew

2 liter(s) of Pink Lemonade

Sugar

6-8 Lemons

6-8 Limes

6-8 Oranges

Directions

Mix the wine with a mixture of the two sodas and pink lemonade.

Squeeze the juice from 2 limes, 2 lemons and 2 oranges (discard squeezed fruit)

Cut the remaining fruit into wedges or wheels.

You'll place ¾ of the remaining fruit into the sangria mix and save the remaining fruit for garnishes on the pitcher and on the glass rims.

Let the pitchers of sangria chill in the refrigerator for one to three hours before serving.

You can make this as a "lite" version by using sugar free soda and sugar free pink lemonade. You can then substitute Splenda for the sugar.

Strawberry & Basil Sangria

You may be thinking Basil? This sangria offers a light summery taste. It's made in this recipe using a rosé wine but you can use other wine too. Personally, I also like it with Moscato wine.

Ingredients

2 bottles rosé wine chilled

1/2 cup Limoncello

1 cup strawberries, washed and sliced

½ cup additional strawberries washed and left whole for garnishing

20 basil leaves washed and dried (you will use 10-12 in sangria and save remaining for garnishing)

Finely grated zest of 1 lemon, plus 1 lemon, thinly sliced, for garnish

1/4 cup lemonade

Directions

Add all ingredients to a sangria pitcher except wine, lemon slices and basil and strawberries that you are holding back for garnish.

Refrigerate 2-3 hours.

When you are ready to serve, stir in the wine and gently mix.

Pour into glasses that are filled ¼ full of ice. Garnish with whole strawberries, remaining basil leaves and lemon slices. Serve.

Strawberry and basil sangria looks a pretty as a picture on your table.

White Sangria

1 Bottle of white wine (chilled)

2/3 cup white sugar

4 oranges (sliced) or may substitute 1 cup of orange juice

3 lemons (sliced)

3 limes (sliced)

2 oz. brandy (optional)

3 peaches sliced (optional)

1/2 liter of ginger ale or club soda

Directions

Pour wine in the pitcher and squeeze the juice wedges from the orange, lemon and lime into the wine, add brandy if desired.

Toss in the fruit wedges and add sugar. Chill 2-6 hours (you can chill overnight if you are making for a party the next day).

Add ginger ale or club soda just before serving.

I like this recipe best with peaches included but it is an optional choice.

Pink Sangria

This sangria is one of my top favorites – nice and light. It's great to serve in a punch bowl at showers too.

Ingredients

2 (750 milliliter) bottles white Zinfandel (chilled)

2 (10 ounce) packages frozen sliced strawberries, thawed

1 (12 fluid ounce) can frozen pink lemonade concentrate, thawed

2 cups pineapple juice

1 liter ginger ale chilled

Directions

Stir the strawberries, lemonade concentrate, rose wine, and pineapple juice in a punch bowl until combined. Stir in the ginger ale just before serving.

You do not want to make this too far in advance as the strawberries may start to get a bit discolored if they sit too long in the mixture.

Traditional Red Sangria

Many sangria recipes call for brandy. Personally, I'm not a brandy person and I often leave it out of my sangria recipes. I don't want the fresh fruit taste smothered by brandy. I suggest if you are adding brandy to use it sparingly, you can always add up to the suggested amount as needed.

Ingredients

1 (750 milliliter) bottle dry red wine (chilled)
1/2 cup brandy
1/4 cup lemon juice
1/3 cup frozen lemonade concentrate
1/3 cup orange juice
1/2 cup triple sec
1 lemon, sliced into rounds
1 orange, sliced into rounds
1 lime, sliced into rounds
1/4 cup white sugar (optional)
1/2 small jar maraschino cherries (you'll use about 12-15 cherries)
2 cups carbonated water or ginger ale (optional)

Directions

In a large pitcher or bowl, mix together the brandy, lemon juice, lemonade concentrate, orange juice, red wine, triple sec, and sugar. Float slices of lemon, orange and lime, and maraschino cherries in the mixture. Refrigerate at least 4 hours. For fizzy sangria, add club soda or ginger ale just before serving.

Mixed Berry Limoncello Sangria

Ingredients

2 (750 milliliter) bottles sparkling wine, chilled
1 cup fresh raspberries
1 cup halved fresh strawberries
½ cup fresh blackberries
1 medium lemon, thinly sliced
½ 12 ounce can frozen pink lemonade concentrate, thawed (3/4 cup)
½ cup (4 ounces) Limoncello (lemon-flavor liqueur)

Directions

In a large pitcher combine raspberries, strawberries, blackberries, and lemon slices. Stir in lemonade concentrate and Limoncello.

Cover and refrigerate for 4 – 6 hours.

Just before serving, add the sparkling wine. Serve in a glass over ice. Garnish the glass with raspberries and / or strawberries.

Note – as you are working with two bottles of wine – you may wish to put half of the berry mix above in one pitcher and half in the other. Then when you are ready to serve a pitcher, add the sparkling wine. When you are ready to serve the second pitcher, add the remaining bottle of sparkling wine.

Berries have a tendency to get "icky" looking if they are in the sangria too long. So rather than have berries disintegrating before your guests eyes, I suggest splitting the recipe in half.

Berry Sangria

Ingredients

1 bottle red wine (chilled)
3/4 cup berry liqueur
1/8 cup white sugar
1 lb. (total) strawberries and/or blueberries (washed)
1/3 lb. seedless grapes (washed)

Directions

Slice the grapes in half and place in a non- metal bowl.
Press ½ of the sugar into the grapes.
Pour ½ of the berry liqueur over the grapes and sugar mixture.
Set aside for 15 – 30 minutes
Place the grape mixture in a sangria pitcher and pour red wine over.
Place in refrigerator for 2-5 hours
Just before serving, put berries in a non -metal bowl. Cut strawberries in half first.
The blueberries can go into the mix as whole berries.
Lightly press remaining sugar into berries and add remaining berry liqueur. Lightly stir and let sit for 5 minutes.
Add berry mix to the pitcher of sangria and lightly stir.
You can garnish the glasses with berries if you choose.
Serve

Simple & Easy White Sangria Recipe

Ingredients

1 bottle white wine (chilled)
3/4 cup Triple Sec
1/8 cup white sugar
1 pound (total) of any combination of these – peaches, oranges, strawberries, limes, lemons (washed)
1/3 lbs. seedless grapes (washed)

Directions

Slice the grapes in half.
If you are using strawberries, slice them in half.
All other fruit should be cut in to wedges.
Place the fruit in a non- metal bowl and gently press the sugar into it. Stir gently to ensure all pieces have sugar on them.
Pour the Triple Sec over the fruit and stir gently.
Cover the bowl and set aside for 15-30 minutes.
Place fruit mixture in a sangria pitcher.
Pour wine over fruit and place in refrigerator for 3 to 5 hours.
Serve and enjoy.

Pineapple Coconut Sangria

Ingredients
1 bottle (750 ml) white wine (chilled)
1 cup coconut rum
1/2 cup mango rum
2 cups pineapple juice
1/2 cup frozen limeade concentrates
Fresh pineapple – cored and cut into small chunks
3 oranges cut into wedges or wheels
½ lbs. seedless grapes (washed) and cut in half

Directions
Combine liquid ingredients in sangria pitcher.
Add fruit, leaving some fruit out for glass garnishes.
Pour over ice in glasses, garnish and serve.

Frozen Peach Sangria

Ingredients
1 (750-ml) bottle white wine (chilled)
3 tablespoons frozen orange juice
1 tablespoon limeade, frozen concentrate
1 cup peach nectar
1 teaspoon vanilla extract
3 tablespoons honey
Sliced fresh peaches for garnish

Directions
Combine all ingredients in a glass mixing bowl and whisk to blend.
Pour into a 9x13 glass baking dish and freeze for at least 3 – 4 hours. Stir hourly.
Once 3-4 hours have passed and your mixture has a chunky consistency,
you will pour in to glasses, garnish and serve

Frozen Sangria
(Party size amount makes 24 servings)

Ingredients
1 gallon sangria (chilled)
1 (12-oz.) can froze limeade, thawed
1 (2-liter) bottle lemon-lime soda
2 cups sliced oranges, lemons, and limes

Directions
 Place 1 2 gallon size zip-top plastic freezer bag inside another 2-gallon zip-top plastic freezer bag. Place bags in a large bowl.

Combine sangria, limeade, and lemon-lime soft drink in the inside bag.

Seal both bags, and freeze 24 hours. (Double bagging is a precaution to avoid spills.)

Remove mixture from freezer 1 hour before serving, squeezing occasionally until slushy.

Transfer mixture to a 2 gallon container. Stir in fruit.

Pour into glasses, garnish and serve.

Non Alcoholic Version Frozen Sangria
Party size (makes up to 24 servings)

Ingredients
1 gallon Cranberry juice cocktail, chilled (you can also use Cranberry/Cherry, Cranberry/Grape versions)
1 (12-oz.) can frozen limeade, thawed
1 (2-liter) bottle lemon-lime soda
2 cups sliced oranges, lemons, and limes

Directions
Place 1 2 gallon size zip-top plastic freezer bag inside another 2 gallon zip-top plastic freezer bag. Place bags in a large bowl.

Combine cranberry juice, limeade, and lemon-lime soft drink in the inside bag.

Seal both bags, and freeze 24 hours. (Double bagging is a precaution to avoid spills.)

Remove mixture from freezer 1 hour before serving, squeezing occasionally until slushy.

Transfer mixture to a 2-gal. container. Stir in fruit.

Non Alcoholic Green Tea Citrus Sangria

Ingredients
4 cups boiling water
3 cups assorted fruit (sliced kiwi and/or plums, raspberries and/or blackberries)
2 cups chilled white cranberry juice
6 Lipton® Green Tea with Citrus Tea Bags
2 Tbsp. honey

Directions
Pour boiling water over Lipton® Green Tea with Citrus Tea Bags in teapot; cover and brew 3 minutes.
Remove Tea Bags and squeeze; stir in honey.

Combine brewed tea with remaining ingredients in pitcher. Chill at least 2 hours.

Serve in ice-filled glasses.

Closing

Thank you for reading my Summertime Sangria book.

Please visit www.LoeraPublishingLLC.com for more book choices.

You are welcome to follow me on Twitter too @99CentsKindle

Made in the USA
Las Vegas, NV
22 July 2022